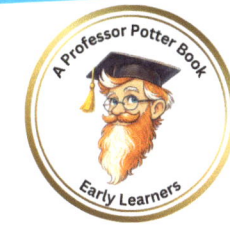

Aa Bb Cc

Professor Potter

Copyright © 2026 by Storytime, LLC.

All rights reserved. No portion of this publication may be reproduced, distributed, or transmitted in any form or by any means, including photocopying, recording, or other electronic or mechanical methods, without the prior written permission of the publisher, except as permitted by U.S. copyright law.

For Violet

Aa

Acorn

Apple

Bb

Bee

Cc

Cat

Circle

Dd

Dog

Ee

Ear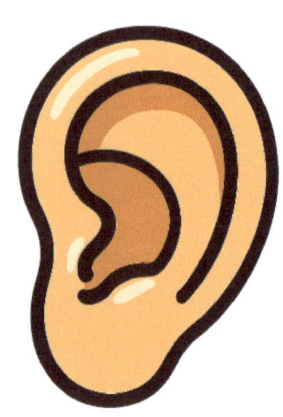

Egg

Ff

Fox

Gg

Goose

Hh

Hat

Ii

Ice Cream

Igloo

Jj

Jeep

King

Ll

Lion

Mm

Monkey

Nn

Nest

Oo

Orange

Octopus

Pp

Pie

Queen

Ring

Ss

Slide

Tt

Turtle

Uu

Unicorn

Violin

Ww

Watch

Xylophone

Yy

Yo-yo

Zz

Zebra

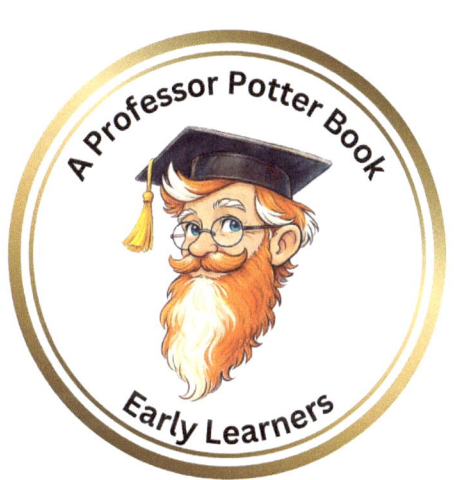

www.ingramcontent.com/pod-product-compliance
Lightning Source LLC
Chambersburg PA
CBHW041135130526
44582CB00031B/133